PORTRAIT OF

Kerala

PORTRAIT OF

Kerala

MELISSA SHALES

PRINCIPAL PHOTOGRAPHY BY

SUNIL VAIDYANATHAN

NH
NEW HOLLAND

First published in 2007 by New Holland Publishers
London • Cape Town • Sydney • Auckland
www.newhollandpublishers.com

86–88 Edgware Road, London, W2 2EA, United Kingdom

80 McKenzie Street, Cape Town, 8001, South Africa

Unit 1, 66 Gibbes Street, Chatswood, NSW 2067, Australia

218 Lake Road, Northcote, Auckland, New Zealand

ISBN 978 1 84537 764 9

Although the publishers have made every effort to ensure that information contained in
this book was correct at the time of going to press, they accept no responsibility
for any inaccuracies, loss, injury or inconvenience sustained
by any person using this book as reference.

Produced for New Holland Publishers (UK) Ltd by

Managing Editor **Mary Anne Evans**
Picture Research **Mary Anne Evans and Melissa Shales**
Senior Editor **Sarah Goulding**
Production **Marion Storz**
Publishing Director **Rosemary Wilkinson**

Reproduction by Pica Digital Pte Ltd
Printed and bound in Malaysia by Tien Wah Press (Pte) Ltd

2 4 6 8 10 9 7 5 3 1

HALF TITLE PAGE *Canoes are the most common form of transport in the Backwaters, while fishermen throw their nets and musselmen dive over the side in search of shellfish.*

TITLE PAGE *Houseboats roofed with coconut matting were once the province of roving bargemen, but are now as likely to be full of tourists living in luxury with an onboard staff.*

THIS PAGE *The children of Kerala will suddenly appear as if from nowhere, masking their huge curiosity about strange foreign visitors with cheeky grins and infectious laughter.*

OVERLEAF *Everything in the Backwaters of Kerala goes by boat, even building materials.*

CONTENTS

KERALA

Parasurama, the sixth avatar (incarnation) of Vishnu and the son of King Jamadagni, received a visit from King Kaartaveerya-arjuna who demanded a sacred cow to feed his army. When Jamadagni refused, the visitors tried to take the cow by force. Parasurama, using the sacred axe which had been given to him by Shiva, killed the entire army. As a reprisal, Kaartaveerya-arjuna beheaded his father, King Jamadagni. But Parasurama was not to be stopped and his sacred axe whirled on, killing Kaartaveerya-arjuna's entire clan in retribution and conquering the world. When he came to the mountains at the edge of the earth he was filled with remorse and did penance. The sea god Varuna saw that his heart was pure and promised to create a new land for him as far as he could throw his axe. Parasuma stood on Gokarnam in the north and hurled the axe along the coast as far as Kanyakumari. From the sea rose Kerala, truly a gift of the gods.

The region has looked towards the sea ever since, cut off from the land by the vast wall of mountains at its back. The caste system, while still based on the three basic divisions of priests, warriors and farmers, was very different to that elsewhere in India. The *nambudiris* (brahmans or priests) had huge power, as any land taken in battle was declared sacred and handed over. In contrast, the *nairs* (warriors) traditionally had matriarchal inheritance law as so few of them survived battle, giving women in Kerala today far greater freedom than in much of India. The *thiyas* (farmers) are thought to have arrived from Sri Lanka, bringing with them the coconut palm. Onto Kerala's Hindu roots have been grafted Judaism, Christianity, Communism and many other influences, brought by Egyptians, Phoenicians, Chinese, Romans, Arabs, Jews, Portuguese, Dutch and British traders over 3,000 years.

RIGHT *There are coconut groves to hang your hammocks at Kappad Beach and an endless expanse of rock and sand to laze on. You can roll in the warm Indian Ocean waves and quench your thirst with the flesh of a tender coconut.*

The Land

Kerala has a coast nearly 580 km (360 miles) long, bordering the Arabian Sea along the southwest shores of India, blessed with many miles of magnificent beaches and some fine natural harbours. The coastal plains are criss-crossed by 44 rivers and huge areas of swamp which have been tamed into a network of lakes, lagoons and canals known as the Backwaters, a land of fish, coconuts and rice paddies. Behind them tower the Western Ghats, reaching heights of 500–2,700 m (1,640–8,858 ft), the lower slopes lush with tea and spice plantations, the higher reaches dense with hardwood jungle.

Kerala covers an area of 38,863 sq km (15,005 sq miles) and has a population of 32 million, of whom about 3.5 million live in the capital, Thiruvananthapuram (Trivandrum). Other major towns include Ernakulam/Kochi (Cochin), Kozikhode (Calicut) and Alapphuza (Alleppey). Many places have changed their names and it pays to know both, as even locals switch them indiscriminately.

The climate is hot and humid on the coast, but cooler and fresher up in the mountains. The monsoon arrives in June for about three months, sweeping across the sea from the southwest in a wall of thick black cloud, with people rushing to the beaches to greet the welcome rains.

LEFT *The Backwaters sustain life on the houseboats, in the coconut groves and rice paddies.*

ABOVE *The Western Ghats stretch off into the dawn from Kadipara Viewpoint in Thekkady.*

RIGHT *Kappad Beach, almost as pristine as the day the gods lifted it from the sea.*

Earliest Inhabitants

To reach back into Kerala's earliest prehistory, head north into the mountains of remote Wayanad province, an area which is still home to many of the tribal people (Paniyas, Adiyas, and Kurichyas) who have survived outside the mainstream of Indian society for thousands of years, literally outcaste, used in the past as slaves or living far off the beaten track. Probably the finest physical evidence of the distant past lies on Ambukuthimala Mountain in the Edakkal Caves (literally 'a stone in between'), a two-chamber cave caused either by earthquake or by Lord Rama's sons, Lava and Kusha, shooting arrows into the earth, depending on which version you prefer. Its walls are covered with three distinct sets of petroglyphs, thought to date back at least 5,000 years. Many are swirling geometric forms, overlaid and confusing, reaching a height of up to 4 m (12.5 ft) and continuing below the level of the modern floor. Others resemble animals including foxes, dogs and an elephant and there are many human figures, some with raised hair, some masked. There are several other known rock art sites, with both engraved pictographs and paintings.

BELOW *Scenes from the life and times of the cave dwellers were meticulously recorded on these walls of the Edakkal Caves. Human figures, animals, and geometric designs compete for attention. Later residents of the cave used hieroglyphs and unknowingly created a language. Five inscriptions have been identified, two of which have been deciphered.*

ABOVE *The caves' walls are covered with linear motifs, making a vertical jumble of congested shallow incisions. Similar straight-line cave drawings (circa 4500 BC) have been found in Stiriya in Europe, and in Africa.*

RIGHT *The Hindu demi god Nandi is Shiva's celestial mount, ensuring that all bulls in India are treated with great respect. No Shiva temple is complete without a Nandi statue standing guard outside the sanctum, alongside live bellowing versions. This early statue is in the Wayanad-Ambylival Museum.*

The Malabar Coast

The Keralan people are Dravidian, believed – with the Tamils in the southeast – to be the aboriginal inhabitants of the subcontinent, and are noticeably smaller, squatter and darker than north Indians. For most of its history, this area was known as the Malabar Coast, after the Arabic/Persian word for the local Malayalam language. Kerala was not one kingdom, but a series of constantly changing small states that spent a considerable amount of time, energy and blood squabbling amongst themselves, totally ignoring the rest of India and concentrating for wealth creation on traders arriving from across the seas. Over this mayhem, the Cheras (who later gave their name to the modern state) held an imperial umbrella for nearly 1,000 years. Most of their building was in wood and there are few physical remains to tell us much about them.

In 664 AD, the first Muslims arrived in the south, converting, unusually, as traders and not by conquest. From the late 10th century, attacks by the Tamil Chola empire grew more intense and while the Cholas never succeeded in taking over Kerala, they did lead to the collapse of the Chera empire, which split into three states: Travangore in the south, Cochin in the centre, and Muslim Calicut in the north. For the most part, Kerala's extraordinary mixed bag of religions – Hindu, Jain, Buddhist, Christian, Jewish and Muslim – survived in perfect harmony until the arrival of the Portuguese, whose fanatical Catholic hatred of Islam unbalanced things in 1498.

BELOW *Tippu's Fort, Palakkad, was built in 1766 by Hyder Ali of Mysore, called in by the Raja of Palakkad to protect him from the Zamorin of Calicut, who was being aided by the British. After being bounced backwards and forwards, under the leadership of Hyder Ali's son, the famous Tippu Sultan, a couple of times, the fort ended up in British hands and was renovated in European style. It is the best preserved fort in Kerala.*

RIGHT *The Trivandrum Padmanabha Swami temple, dedicated to Vishnu, is the largest temple complex in Kerala, consecrated in 1050 AD, although there has been a temple on this site since at least the 6th century AD. It was largely rebuilt after a fire in 1729.*

The Incomers

Drawn here by the promise of ivory, pearls, sandalwood, teak and spices, trading ships have been visiting the Keralan coast for at least 3,000 years. The ancient Egyptians, Phoenicians, Chinese, Romans and Arabs all came and made their mark. The first Jews arrived in 587 BC, finding a home in Cochin after being thrown out by King Nebuchudnezzar. The Apostle Thomas (Doubting Thomas) landed at Cranganore in 52 AD, introducing Syrian Orthodox Christianity.

When Columbus sailed the ocean blue in 1492 and Vasco da Gama set out six years later, it was with one purpose – to find a sea route to the Spice Coast of India and break the Arab monopoly on this precious trade. Vasco's arrival in Calicut (Kozikhode) in 1498 quite literally changed the world. It also changed the Malabar Coast as the Portuguese, British and Dutch piled their military muscle in behind either the Rajas of Cochin or Travancore or Zamorin of Calicut, according to who was most grateful at the time. Meantime, with the Islamic empires of India looking to suck in this rich land, the British became the least of all evils and by the late 18th century, Calicut had become a colony while Travancore and Cochin had puppet governments.

BELOW *St Francis Church was the first European church built in India. Its history chronicles the power struggle between the various European powers that fought for a foothold on the Indian subcontinent. Originally built in wood by the Franciscan friars who came with the Portuguese expedition in 1500 AD, it was enlarged and rebuilt in stone. Portuguese patronage lasted until 1663, when it came under Dutch control and became a Protestant church. Finally, in the nineteenth century the church was handed over to the Anglicans.*

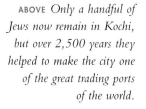

ABOVE *Only a handful of Jews now remain in Kochi, but over 2,500 years they helped to make the city one of the great trading ports of the world.*

RIGHT *The paved road from Munnar to Top Station was constructed in the early 20th century. Before that you had three choices: you could ride a mule, trek 15 km (9 miles), or be carried by bearers in a palanquin if you were a sahib.*

17

Kerala Today

In 1956, the three old principalities of Cochin, Travancore and Calicut were finally linked into the modern state of Kerala, the borders arranged along the linguistic boundary – the three share the Malayalam language. In 1957, Kerala made history by becoming the first place in the world to elect a Communist government in free elections, the hammer and sickle even seen occasionally flying happily on a church roof.

The state's unusual past, with Hinduism, Christianity, Communism, and Islam living relatively peacefully side by side, has had some very obvious benefits. Kerala is noticeably wealthier, cleaner and tidier than much of India, with fewer beggars. The state claims 100 per cent literacy. While this is an exaggeration (the reality is probably a still impressive 91 per cent), education is undoubtedly far better than elsewhere and people are, on the whole, wealthier. Women have far greater rights, birth control has helped to slow India's overwhelming population explosion, and infant mortality, health and life expectancy rates are above the national average.

But problems still exist. People are poor. For all its water, Kerala has faced drought as it battles for water with its neighbours and industry. Pollution threatens the Backwaters, and overfishing is forcing the fishermen ever further off the coast. Crime is relatively high. Many men work away from home in the Middle East, increasing numbers of Tamils are arriving in search of low-paid work in the fields, and the tribal peoples are demanding the return of their traditional land. It isn't paradise, but Kerala is definitely doing something right.

RIGHT *The old and the new – amidst the fishing villages and coconut groves where these children live in Kappad stands a concrete pillar with an inscription marking Vasco da Gama's voyage to India.*

ABOVE *Every street in Kerala has a temple, church, or mosque. In many cases, gods with conflicting ideologies live on the same street.*

LEFT *Kerala has achieved an index of human development comparable to the world's developed countries, largely due to the priority accorded to education. Both sexes have access to primary and secondary schools.*

OVERLEAF *Sheer cliff faces of red laterite give bathers a tame sea and privacy at unspoiled Varkala, where sand castles worthy of science fiction are built.*

THE OCEAN

It's late afternoon and the world is bathed in a golden glow. Take a sip of a masala milkshake with a kick like a mule and a mouthful of fresh pineapple and banana pancakes to wash it down. Wriggle your toes deeper into the sand and wait. It's been a busy day on the beach, Keralan style, starting with a sunrise stroll before breakfast, watching the yoga class from a nearby resort tying themselves in knots. A full South Indian breakfast is followed by an early burst of sunbathing, pulling back into the shade of the palms with cool coconut water in the shell to drink as the heat begins to shimmer across the hot white sand.

A chat with the mussel fishermen can lead to a canoe trip out across the bay, tucking in the toes as the purple jellyfish drift past, holding your breath and counting as the fishermen dive deep to collect the mussels, and shouting as the canoe surfs back into the white sandy beach on a giant wave.

Fresh fish barbecued on the beach for lunch might be followed by an Ayurvedic massage to cleanse the body, leading to an urgent need for pineapple and banana pancakes. Now it's time for sunset and all the local families, street vendors, touts and tourists turn out to watch as the sea and sky burst into amber flame.

BELOW *Five centuries ago, 170 men led by the Portuguese navigator Vasco da Gama (1460–1524) stepped onto the Keralan shore at Kappad (Calicut) and changed history. Today's visitors come for the sea and sand.*

RIGHT *It is not just the beach that attracts tourists to Kappad; many little streams and rivulets meet the sea here, creating this unique wall of green that extends along the length of the beach, within which hide many fascinating traditional fishing villages.*

The Beaches

With hundreds of kilometres of coastline, there are plenty of beaches to choose from in Kerala, but very few have been developed for tourism. Others are fishing villages or used as the local lavatories by communities without sanitation – paradise isn't always all it seems! Of the tourist beaches, by far the best known is Kovalam, once a delightful hippy hangout. It is still delightful, but increasingly busy with mass-market Europeans barbecueing themselves lobster-pink on its three crescents of white sand.

Elsewhere, the 140 year-old pier at Alappuzha (Alleppey) beach is a favourite place from which to watch the spectacular sunsets, while a beach park offers plenty of entertainment for the children. Kappad Beach is where Vasco da Gama and his men first landed in 1498, an event commemorated on the beautiful rocky shoreline with its dense backdrop of coconut groves and rivulets. Classically palm-fringed Bekal Beach offers the opportunity to explore a huge, well-preserved fort on the shore, while dolphins are occasionally seen playing near Cherai Beach. Varkala Beach is the place to chill, famed for its curative mineral springs and special massages. It's also an important pilgrimage centre, with a dip in the holy sea said to cleanse the body and soul of all sin. Less well-known beaches worth exploring include Kappil, Kizhunna Ezhara, Marari (Mararikulam), and Padinharekara.

ABOVE *Discovered by the hippies long before the rest of us, Kerala's beaches typically have small, low-rise hotels and guesthouses hidden amongst the coconut palms, with few mass-market hotels.*

LEFT *Shallow, sloping white sand and warm Indian Ocean waters give Kovalam its idyllic beaches, but it is rapidly becoming overcrowded as a result.*

RIGHT *Yoga on the beach – stress-busting holidays are increasingly popular in Kerala.*

RIGHT *Alleppey Beach is referred to as the 'Venice of the East' by travellers from across the world due to the Backwaters that empty into it. The beachfront is delightful, and offers walkers a fairly long stretch, with an old lighthouse nearby. The sea here is very rough; check with a lifeguard before you plunge into the water, and swim between the red flags.*

OPPOSITE ABOVE *Three school friends here in search of adventure were enjoying their Christmas vacations. They tailed me for some time before mustering the courage to speak, then implored me to take their picture so that their girlfriends could have a visual account of their adventures.*

OPPOSITE BELOW *The Calicut sea front swarms with holiday makers and locals alike and offers every sort of entertainment from ice cream sellers, flute music and amusement rides to majestic views, traditional fishing villages, and glorious solitude. But beware. Late evening walks can be marred by overzealous, drunken fishermen!*

LEFT *Master flute maker and flautist 'Venu' is one of Varkala's star attractions; to find him you just have to follow the sweet music of his Krishna bhajans.*

BELOW *Dancing on Kappad Beach as the sun goes down.*

RIGHT *West-facing Kerala celebrates the sunset with a magnificent spectacle each evening.*

Fishing and Fishermen

The traditional fishing nets are an integral part of Kochi's maritime heritage, but these picture-perfect contraptions and the fisher folk who operate them need immediate help to survive. No visit to Kochi is complete without observing them in action. Unfortunately, the lives of fishermen who operate them are in crisis. Over the years, the catch has reduced drastically due to the environmental impact caused by burgeoning demands on one of India's busiest transhipment ports.

These fishing nets have been here for centuries and are believed to be Chinese in origin. This is not as improbable as the 5,000 km (3,100 mile) distance from China might suggest. Kochi, an important trading post on the spice route, would certainly have attracted Chinese traders. Some believe that the nets may even have been introduced by the famous Chinese admiral and explorer, Zheng He, who made seven voyages of discovery commanding a great Chinese fleet from 1405 to 1433, visiting India on at least three of them.

These nets are fixed land installations with shore-operated lift nets. Huge mechanical contrivances hold out horizontal nets of 20 m (65 ft) or more across. Each structure is at least 10 m (33 ft) high and consists of a cantilever with an outstretched net suspended over the sea, with large stones suspended from ropes as counterweights at the other end. Each installation is operated by a team of up to six fishermen. The system is so finely balanced that the weight of a man walking along the main beam is enough to make the net descend into the sea. The cross beam with the net is submerged for a short time, possibly just a few minutes, before it is raised by pulling the ropes. The catch is usually modest: a few fish and crustacea that are sold to passers-by within minutes.

The system of counterweights is most ingenious. Rocks, each approximately 30 cm (11.7 in) in diameter are suspended from ropes of different lengths. As the net is raised, the rocks slowly come to rest on a platform, keeping everything in balance. Each installation has a limited operating depth. Consequently, an individual net cannot be operated continually in tidal waters. Different installations will be operated depending on the height of the tide. The cost of maintaining these huge contraptions and abysmal profit margins may render these contraptions obsolete very soon.

RIGHT *The catch is a vital source of income for locals.*

FAR RIGHT *The Chinese fishing nets are to Kochi what the gondolas are to Venice. One cannot imagine Kochi's shores without this strange but beautiful contraption that resembles a wooden praying mantis.*

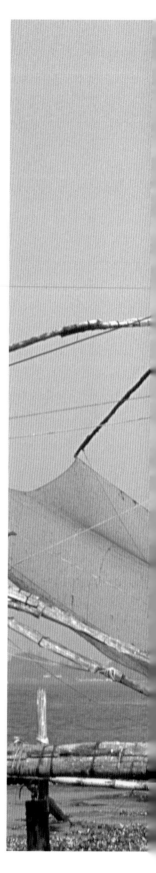

ABOVE *After the last few entangled fishes have been removed, the nets are checked for damage before being folded neatly for the next fishing session.*

LEFT *Once each catch has been brought in, the fishermen immediately mend their own nets with real skill and manual dexterity.*

RIGHT *Many Chinese fishing nets are now redundant; the fishermen who own these nets earn more money from 'baksheesh' than from the actual catch. The polluted shipping channel cannot sustain a healthy ecosystem, and the locals are forced to venture into deep sea.*

BELOW *Among fishing communities women have an important part to play, as the responsibility of men ends with bringing the catch home. After that, they are free to pursue their favourite pastime of drinking and card games while distributing and selling the fish falls to the women.*

LEFT *As the sun goes down, the necks of the fishing nets continue to duck and bob, lights hanging from the bamboo frames to entice the fish to the surface. For tourists, the silhouette against the sunset is one of the great sights of Kochi.*

THE BACKWATERS

The Backwaters of Kerala are an unmissable sight, with 3,200 sq km (1,235 sq miles) of tranquil lagoons and shady canals stretching languidly along the coast and inland as 44 rivers tumble off the Western Ghats down to the sea, looping across the coastal plains as they go. At the centre of Kerala, Vembanad Lake – along with the adjacent wetlands over the eastern and southern sides – forms Kuttanad, 'the rice bowl of Kerala', and the largest wetlands system on the western coast of India. Five rivers originating in the Western Ghats drain into this lake, which originally covered a vast 350 sq km (135 sq miles). A large area of this was reclaimed to provide agricultural land, shrinking the lake to less than 200 sq km (77 sq miles), while the narrow strips of water between the paddy fields became the Backwaters. A good portion of these wetlands has been converted into paddy fields, which remain waterlogged for six months a year. Some areas are left fallow throughout the year. With canals in place of roads, journeying by boat is the only way of getting around, and offers a unique glimpse of the importance water plays in the locals' lives.

Take a boat trip from the ancient port of Kollam (Quilon) across palm-fringed lakes and along canals where the silence may be broken by the gentle dance of water birds wading in the shallows, the splash of otters playing, or the bustle of coir (coconut fibre) and copra (dried coconut flesh) being loaded onto boats. Here, nature mingles with village life as narrow spits of reclaimed land house tiny settlements where children learn to swim as soon as they can walk, messing around in canoes while their fathers fish and their mothers work bent over double in the rice paddies.

Choose from a tourist cruise, take the local ferry or push the boat out and rent a *kettuvalam* (rice barge houseboat) and spend your days unwinding, and your nights under a blanket of stars. Search the shoreline for kingfishers and kites along the shore at the Kumarakom bird sanctuary, and make a pilgrimage to nearby Amrithapuri, the residence of Matha Amrithanandamayi, 'The Hugging Mother', and one of India's few female gurus. Climb ashore at Kollam and Alapphuzha (Alleppey) to explore their rich heritage of temples and old colonial buildings, cashew nut and coir factories.

RIGHT *The endless expanse of azure, fluffy white and green reflected on the surface of Vembanad Lake is so still that you need to dip your feet to check if it is real or a 19th-century engraving.*

ABOVE *Hundreds of houseboats are anchored opposite the Nehru Pavilion on Vembanad Lake. Houseboat owners and their agents will cajole you, each describing the virtues of their boat, and occasionally warning you as to why their competitor's vessel cannot be trusted.*

LEFT *Pretty pictures can be deceptive. It costs two hundred thousand Indian rupees to build a three-bedroom houseboat, and a small fraction of that to power it with a leaking outboard. Houseboat owners and tourists must look to environmental concerns or face disaster.*

RIGHT *The houseboats operated by the Kerala Tour Company boast three spacious bedrooms with en-suite bathrooms, and a dining area that provides a panoramic view.*

BELOW *Tourist houseboats also come with a full complement of staff including a team of chefs who can serve up everything from Kerala cuisine to continental food.*

LEFT *While some live on the water, other Backwater villagers live precariously balanced on the narrow dykes between the canals and the rice paddies.*

BELOW *The lifeblood of the Backwaters people are the boats that ply their trade here, used for housing, transport, commuting, commerce and, in recent times, pleasure. As boatman Unnikrishnan puts it: "We were born on the lake; how can we imagine life without our boats?"*

RIGHT *The ferry from Alleppey to Kottayam offers great views of Vembanad Lake and Kumarakonam Bird Sanctuary.*

LEFT *A boy rows to school in Kuttinad district. Children are at home on and in the water, often learning to swim before they can walk.*

RIGHT *Fishing from a canoe in the Backwaters takes some degree of skill and balance to throw the net successfully without falling in yourself.*

BELOW *Multi-tasking – doing the washing up in the lagoon while having a bath. The lagoon provides the locals with everything they need.*

Bananas

Fourteen different varieties of banana are cultivated in Kerala, from the sweet and yellow to the savoury green plantain and the strange looking red banana or *nendraparam*. They grow all over the state, commercially, in gardens and even at the entrance to temples where they are considered auspicious and are used in religious ceremonies, such as weddings.

Every part of the plant (actually a giant herb) is used. The bananas themselves are eaten raw or cooked, sweet or savoury, curried or fried. Try banana milkshakes and pancakes, dried banana and above all, banana crisps. The purple flowers and soft inner trunk are also eaten as vegetables, while the leaves, which can be up to 3 m (10 ft) long and 60 cm (2 ft) wide, are used for weaving, as thatch and even as plates.

The 'trunk' of the plant, which can reach heights of up to 10 m (33 ft), is actually made up of tightly wrapped leaf sheaths. Each flowering head produces a stem of up to 300 fruit. These are rich in carbohydrates and low in fat, providing potassium and vitamins B6 and C. They are excellent for providing energy and helping the digestion, and they are also said to help fight depression, baldness and muscle cramps.

BELOW *The cultivators bring their produce to a central market in Trissur where commission agents haggle over prices. After the bananas are sorted according to size, then weighed, they are dispatched to wholesalers throughout the country.*

RIGHT *King of the bananas — a labourer piles bananas high on a truck in Trissur's fruit market.*

Coir

The commercial production of coir in Kerala dates back to the 19th century, since when it has grown to become the largest cottage industry in the state, employing over a million people. Coir spinning wheels were introduced in the middle of the 19th century to increase production and obtain the required yarn strength for the manufacture of matting.

To prepare coir yarn on the spinning wheel, one set of two wheels, one stationary and the other movable, is required. The stationary wheel usually contains two spindles set in motion through the centre of the wheel. The movable wheel contains one spindle. Two people take the slivers of 'coir' prepared and kept ready after willowing. Usually women keep them in their armpits, make a loop with a small quantity of fibre and then put the loop thus formed into the notch of one of the spindles on the stationary wheel, which gives the fibre a uniform thickness while walking backwards. Traditional spinning using a spinning wheel requires three people, who can produce up to 15 kg (33 lb) of yarn per day.

In Alleppey, you can see coconut husks being beaten into fibre for making beautiful mats and other coir products. In more recent years, environmentally friendly, coir-based products are being used instead of peat as garden fertilizer and for carpets in western homes.

BELOW *Made from the hairy husk of the coconut, coir is not only an essential for local life but a thriving Keralan export. Alleppey (Alappuzha in Malayalam) is the nerve centre of the industry.*

ABOVE *Both men and women work in the industry, women spinning the yarn while the men weave it into products.*

RIGHT *The painstakingly spun yarn is then rolled into huge balls and transported to factories in Alleppey for further processing.*

Rice

The wet, tropical state of Kerala, with its annual rainfall of about 300 cm (117 in), is ideal for the cultivation of one of the world's great staples. Rice is typically grown on small farms of between 0.4–2 hectares (1–5 acres) in the terraced valleys between the rolling green hills and the coastal plains, where water drains off after the monsoons. It is a good crop, resistant to disease and pests and, in some areas of the country, it produces two harvests a year.

Rice paddies full of workers bent over the slender grasses are a picturesque sight. And they don't just provide employment – they have also become an important habitat for all kinds of birds from herons to warblers, as well as a wide variety of amphibians and snakes, which act as natural pest controllers.

Surprisingly, Kerala has always had to import rice, and farmers are still turning away from growing the staple in favour of more profitable cash crops. But Kerala's other great and increasingly important revenue earner, Ayurvedic medicine, is unexpectedly boosting rice producion. The Njavara strain of rice which is only grown in Kerala has always been important as a natural therapy. For native Keralans, a kind of porridge, made from Njavara grains and mixed with herbs to make an effective health drink, is traditionally consumed during the month of Karkkidakun (July and August). At Ayurvedic centres, the classic way of treating rheumatism and neural disorders is to paste the whole body with Njavara rice grains cooked in milk. Apparently, it does the trick.

RIGHT *Harvesting rice in the Kuttinad district. It isn't strictly necessary to plant rice in paddy fields, but the shallow waters help to keep away the weeds before the rice plants settle in. Cultivating it is a backbreaking exercise done, for the most part, bent over double.*

SPICES AND FOOD

Spices are integral to Kerala's history. It was the prospect of trade in that precious commodity that brought the ancient Phoenicians here. Much later, in 1498, Vasco da Gama, seeking the sea route to India to capture the spice trade, introduced five centuries of European influence in India. Many of the aromatic spices that were so sought after in Europe to flavour food and wine and preserve meat were, and still are, grown in Kerala. They were carried down to the Malabar Coast, then transported thousands of miles by boat, camel and cart to a continent that would pay heavily for the hot tastes from exotic Asia.

Today, many spices are grown in the Cardamom Hills near the Periyar Wildlife Sanctuary, where various companies offer visitors tours of the spice plantations and the chance to overnight at one as well. But whether staying on a plantation or just travelling around the region, the pungent smells and the bright colours of the spices mount a continuous, intoxicating assault on your senses. The sharp, bright yellow of turmeric clashes with the scarlet chillies, and the rich fragrance of cloves battle with cardamom, making a heady mix.

Pepper, the 'King of Spices' was vital to medieval Europe; today local Keralan varieties like 'Malabar Garbled' and 'Tellicherry Extra Bold' are considered the best in culinary world terms. The 'Queen of Spices', cardamom, used as a flavouring in baking for centuries, cinnamon, once more precious than gold, and ginger, valued for its preservative and medicinal properties, today grow alongside more recently introduced plants such as vanilla and nutmeg – grown on trees imported from Indonesia's Spice Islands, and the European staple flavours of oregano, rosemary, thyme and sage.

The main pepper market is now centred in Kochi's Jewtown, offering a kind of Dickensian India where little, including the spice trade, has changed over the centuries.

BELOW LEFT *Dried ginger and cinnamon are widely used in south Indian cuisine. The potent antioxidant properties of cinnamon extends the shelf life of foods and aids in digestion, while dried ginger has been alleged to cure everything from colds to impotency.*

RIGHT *Most markets in Kerala have a separate section dedicated to spices. You do not have to ask for directions; just follow your nose…*

The Basic Ingredients of Life

Mention Kerala, and three basic ingredients come to mind. With such an abundance of salt and fresh water, it is hardly suprising that fish is the first one. The fish on display in the pungently smelling market in Kochi or in baskets in the fishing boats down by the harbour ranges from the usual Indian bluey-grey pomfret to huge crayfish, crabs, giant eel and the prawns for which Kochi is famous. The second basic ingredient is rice, which is present at every meal, while the third part of the culinary puzzle is the ubiquitous coconut.

Coconut trees line the roadways and form the backdrop to the lush beaches and the slow-moving, green backwaters. Growing to around 25 m (75 ft), and topped with long, feather-like leaves, the oval-shaped nuts grow in bunches high up the trunk. Each tree produces 50 to 100 nuts a year, and nothing is wasted either from the fruit or from the tree itself. Coconut beams hold up traditional houses; the leaves thatch the roofs and are used to weave mats and baskets; the husk produces coir; and the shell is turned into spoons and ladles.

Stop at the roadside and small boys run up with green coconuts to sell, the outer skin taken off and a straw stuck in the top to suck the juice out. The flesh is used in curries and sweetmeats, and coconut flesh is creamed and mixed with water. Coconut oil is used extensively in cooking and the dessicated flesh, or copra, is dried and kept for the frying pan, as well as being used as offerings in temples.

RIGHT *As fishermen display their catch to prospective buyers, a cat patiently looks on, hoping for a share.*

LEFT *Coconut climbers are much sought after in Kerala, and the state even boasts a coconut climbing school and a coconut tree-climbing championship.*

Cooking

Keralan cooking is very different from the richer, heavier tradition of north India. The southern cuisine is relatively simple; it's also healthy and using very little oil, it reflects the state's emphasis on Ayurvedic medicine. With such an abundance of fresh ingredients, there is little need for complicated cooking or heavy saucing.

Kerala's history and its long coastline have brought Hindu, Christian and Muslim influences, all of which are evident in the state's cuisine. Christian influence comes with stews of chicken, duck and goat (lamb is almost completely unknown), dry meat curries with shredded coconut, and spicy stewed fish. From the Arabs came *pathiri*, a pancake made of rice flour, and *alsa*, a traditional Arabic dish of wheat, chicken and salt. Vegetarian cooking is very widespread, the dishes often highly spiced.

Kerala is also known for its traditional *sadhyas*, a vegetarian meal served on a banana leaf with boiled rice and various side dishes. It is followed by *payasam*, a sweet milk dessert. There are differences within the state: the south Kerala dishes are spiced up with garlic, which is missing in the north. Keralan fish curry is deservedly well known, as is the Keralan variety of *parathas*, flatbread stuffed with vegetables and renowned throughout India.

BELOW *A freshly caught crayfish quickly fried in coconut oil makes for a feast.*

ABOVE *'Idlis' or rice dumplings feature on the menu of every roadside eatery in Kerala. They are safe as long as you avoid the 'chatni' which is a ground concoction of coconut kernel, green chillies, and un-boiled water.*

ABOVE RIGHT AND RIGHT *The 'idlis' are made by putting rice batter in moulds and steaming it in a closed dish.*

PEOPLE

A woman glides out from beneath the palm trees with a basket of pineapples, a broad smile on her face and huge knife in one hand. As she squats on the sand and deftly slices up a fresh fruit salad, she talks of her day that started with cutting the fruit in the fields at 4am before getting a bus to spend the day selling it to the tourists.

Life is very different here than in many parts of India after years of socialist rule. Women in Kerala generally have a much better life – more freedom, equality under the law and in society and fewer children – but making a living still involves a great deal of hard work. With high standards of education, people are extremely politically aware, with more newspapers here than in any other part of the country. Many of the men work in the Middle East while workers flood in from Tamil Nadu to take on the unskilled jobs.

Even physically, the people in Kerala are very different to the north Indians – shorter, squatter, darker, their faces rounder and broader, the descendants of the aboriginal Dravidians not the Aryan invaders. They speak a different language, Malayalam. They are gentler, less aggressive and more solemn, until it comes to festival time when they kick up a storm of dazzling colour and sound to make the heavens tremble.

RIGHT *A pilgrim walks past the wheel of a juggernaut – a giant chariot used during important Hindu festivals to take the gods on a tour of the city in Suchindram.*

BELOW *The joys of spring – something had really made the day of this schoolgirl at Vembanad Lake.*

ABOVE *In Kerala, food is generally served on banana leaves; fresh leaves are collected and washed before serving dinner.*

RIGHT *The shredded coconut husk has to be finely threshed before spinning it into yarn. Groups of women strike the heaps of husk with sticks till the fibres separate.*

BELOW *Women take a lift to work in a truck. Poverty and lack of employment opportunities in nearby Tamil Nadu force many families to migrate to bigger cities in search of work. These women were lucky, as a road project on the Tamil Nadu–Kerala border will ensure at least three months of employment.*

OPPOSITE *This young boy was very apprehensive; it took a whole bar of chocolate to make him smile.*

BELOW LEFT *Pilgrims queue up at the Sri Krishna Temple at Guruvayoor for a glimpse of their favourite god Krishna, 'the frivolous flautist' who is so dear to every Indian.*

RIGHT *This young pilgrim was blissfully unaware of events.*

BELOW *The stuffed toy puppy was apparently very ill, and was being treated by the elder sister when her brother turned up and argued about the best course of treatment.*

LEFT *A fisherman, Joseph, at Bekal Beach, during a mid-morning hooch-tasting session and an impromptu song about the sea.*

ABOVE *Tribal people, who once poached in the Periyar Reserve, are now employed as forest guards and trackers, while eco-development committees in the surrounding villages aim to make the communities less dependant on forest resources.*

RIGHT *As is the case with all places of pilgrimage in India, Guruvayoor has its own share of resident beggars, who help the pilgrims score extra karma points.*

STREET LIFE

City streets come as quite a shock after the serene Keralan countryside with their traffic jams and blasting horns, auto-rickshaws buzzing like angry wasps and chanting street vendors selling newspapers and soft drinks, *idlis* and *upattam*, their voices a high incomprehensible chant. Larger shops with plate glass windows proudly display the latest fashions from Mumbai and Delhi; smaller backstreet tailors sit surrounded by bales of fabric, ready to make a copy in a couple of hours. High-pitched pop music and the low call of a sacred cow mingle with the chatter of men in business suits and market traders.

Ernakulam/Kochi is a double-sided city, with modern Ernakulam on the mainland, and the historic island of Fort Kochi (Cochin) – where much more of the past survives in the cobbled streets of Jewtown, the aromas of the spice market and the Chinese fishing nets along the seafront. The only real city in Kerala is the capital, Thiruvananthapuram (Trivandrum), thought to be the fabled city of Ophir, where King Solomon traded for spices 1000 years BC. It was, more recently, capital of the princely state of Travancore, but while it bustles with its own importance and is home to Kerala's largest temple, the Sri Padmanabhaswami temple, it shows little sign now of its ancient past, far more concerned with getting on with the future.

BELOW *Trivandrum Fort is the business district of the capital, Thiruvananthapuram.*

ABOVE RIGHT *Umbrella sellers are everywhere – even at the entrance to a temple.*

BELOW RIGHT *Malayalam films fall into four categories: super throbbing (just short of soft porn), mind throbbing (voluptuous actor in body-hugging clothes), super action thriller (guns and bleeding villains), and super romantic (fully dressed actors in a flowery bed).*

Kochi (Cochin)

The first 'black' Jews arrived in 587 BC, thrown out of their homeland by King Nebuchudnezzar. Over the centuries they intermarried, but some remained true to the Jewish religion. A second wave of 'white' Jews arrived in around 1000 AD. This time, the community closed in on itself, remaining close-knit, living together, intermarrying and working as spice traders in Cranganore.

With the arrival of the Portuguese, anti-Jewish sentiment was stirred up and they fled south to Kochi where they were given a grant of land to build a settlement and synagogue. Jewtown, as it quickly became known, remained a centre of the spice trade right up until the end of World War II, when many of the community moved to Israel. Now only about thirteen Jews remain in Kochi. The air is still scented by the spice market nearby, but where it would once have been bustling with ox-carts filled with sacks of pepper, cinnamon and vanilla, Jewtown Street itself is now almost solely the province of tourists as they visit the synagogue and cemetery, stopping to buy antiques and souvenirs, coffee and, of course, spices.

BELOW *A fish seller rides past a row of shops in Jewtown.*

ABOVE RIGHT *The Jewish Synagogue at Mattanchery was built in 1568, making it the oldest in the Commonwealth. Its simple exterior hides an elaborate interior with exquisite hand-painted Chinese tiles.*

BELOW RIGHT *The thirteen remaining Jews that call Jewtown their home have zealously guarded their way of life. There is a little board painted in yellow and post-box red which warns prospective buyers of imposters.*

LEFT *Framed pictures of gods and goddesses are popular with the pious. Every Indian household will have a little niche dedicated to their favourite gods. A prayer session (puja) is held twice a day to appease the gods and ask for the family's welfare. The most popular deities are Ganesha, Laxmi, the goddess of wealth, and Krishna, the eternal romantic.*

BELOW LEFT *Gods are hard to please; little roadside shops like these sell karma multipliers in the form of floral tributes, lamps, idols, tap water in brass containers ('from the Ganges'), and bells and cymbals to rouse the gods from their eternal slumber.*

ABOVE *Life's a beach and everywhere there's the opportunity for a sale – even if it's selling whirling paper windmills off the back of a bicycle on Fort Kochi's foreshore.*

RIGHT *Son of Parvati and Shiva, the elephant-headed god, Ganesha, is the most popular in the Hindu pantheon – the lord of prosperity and good fortune and the clearer of obstacles.*

Transport

Transport in Kerala is a whole world of entertainment and adventure in itself. With a little ingenuity, you can get anywhere on public transport and you will have a wonderful time. Trains clatter down the coast, linking Kerala with the rest of India. In the rural bus stations, you are reliant on the kindness of a small child or an old lady to point you in the right direction, with every sign written in a different alphabet and not an English speaker in sight. Crowded onto the bus, in pride of place on the engine housing, you just cross your fingers and hope you are going the right way – or that you will like wherever it is that it takes you to.

On the Backwaters, there simply are no roads. A network of government ferries criss-crosses the canals and lagoons, offering an excellent way to spend the day exploring the area for a fraction of the price of an official tour. You may well be invited up onto the roof to chat to the engineer and captain, and may even get taken home to tea in one of the tiny knife-edge hamlets perched on the dykes between the paddy fields. Ask nicely and the fishermen will be happy to take you out in their canoes, or if you want to do things in style, hire a houseboat.

Back on land, if you want to play it safe there are, of course, plenty of taxis and hire cars and comfortable coaches that will whisk you wherever you want to go in air-conditioned ease.

ABOVE *Lorries are brightly decorated and often covered with pithy sayings or words of wisdom.*

LEFT *A Kerala Transport Corporation bus passes under the gateway of Trivandrum Fort, where most of the commercial businesses and many good eateries are to be found.*

LEFT *Only recommended for the adventurous with a strong arm, these little row boats provide the ideal romantic getaway. You can even explore the metre-wide canals that lead into the villages. A word of caution though: when the big houseboats pass, hold tight or row fast. The wake makes the little boats bob up and down violently.*

BELOW *Local children enjoy a weekend outing on the canals.*

A FEELING OF WELLBEING

Taken from two Sanskrit words, *ayus* (long life) and *veda* (knowledge), even the name of Ayurveda promises a lot. This form of healing is known to have been in use in the Indian subcontinent when Buddha was alive (around 520 BC) and is probably far older than that, although treatments have continued to progress over the years.

To Ayurvedic practictioners, life is made up of four essential parts: the mind, body, senses and soul. Each person contains five elements – air, fire, earth, water and space (ether). Ether and air together make up the *Vata dosha*, which governs movement, from the circulation of the blood to the nervous system that controls our muscles. Fire and water together make up the *Pitta dosha* or metabolism. Water and earth combine to create the *Kapha dosha* which dictates growth and protection within the body. For perfect health, all these systems must be in alignment.

This state of alignment is produced by a regimen of medicines created from herbs and minerals, along with massage and oil therapies. Kerala, as a state, is a firm believer in Ayurvedic treatments and has developed many of its own remedies for diseases from asthma to ulcers. Or you can just lie back and unwind on a carpet of flowers, and allow the healing powers of Keralan rice and expert massage waft you into total relaxation.

LEFT *The Taj Green Cove Resort and Spa in Kovalam is the place for a perfect, relaxing holiday.*

ABOVE *This type of therapy is used for stress management. A mix of liquids including herbal oils, medicated milk and butter is poured on the forehead in a special rhythm for about 45 minutes a day for 7 to 21 days.*

RIGHT *The treatment of feet is one of the classic therapies offered at the Taj Green Cove Resort and Spa in Kovalam.*

LEFT *Stress management therapy is particularly used to treat insomnia, mental tension, mental stress and certain skin diseases.*

BELOW *Body massage with herbal oils by hand tones up the body and dramatically improves circulation.*

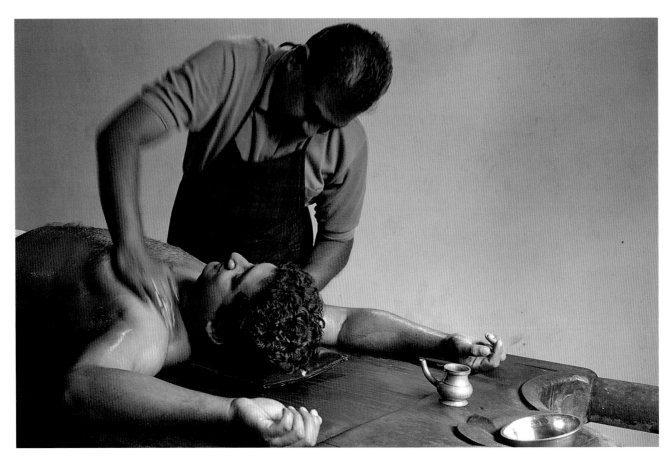

RIGHT AND BELOW LEFT
Ayurvedic treatments and therapies use natural ingredients, fresh fruit, vegetables and oil at the Taj Malabar Cochin Resort.

BELOW RIGHT *There is nothing more soothing than a classic Indian head massage.*

HILL STATIONS

Anyone who lives in the heat and has the money for a second home in the hills will move as summer turns up the dial and the monsoon draws in the mosquitoes. The rajas commuted to the hills long before the arrival of the British, who created a real feel of an English country garden in many of the hill stations. Today, the British are long gone but the hill stations still have a cosy quaintness, Indian-style, with lush botanic gardens, lakes and waterfalls, picnic spots and views. They are also the ideal place in which to base yourself comfortably while trekking in the hills, and each of them has its own distinctive draw. Of them all, Munnar is the most famous, surrounded by thousands of hectares of tea plantations. Wayanad is home to the extraordinary Edakkal Caves and several fine temples, and is also the area where many of the tribal people live if you wish to explore this different, older way of life. Idukki offers tribal people, spice tours and elephant rides.

PREVIOUS PAGES *Manicured tea estates fold across the Munnar landscape. As you turn, the landscape follows, like a seamless cyclorama.*

BELOW *Walk along any of the narrow hill roads that skirt the tea gardens and you are bound to come across little Victorian bungalows that were once home to the 'sahibs'. The sahibs still live here; the only difference is that today's tea estate managers are Indians.*

RIGHT *Tamil labourers brought from Tamil Nadu, and their successors, now form a majority in Munnar. In this part of Kerala everyone speaks Tamil, and the tea workers live in small semi-permanent structures that fringe the tea gardens.*

BELOW *Tamils love loud colours and this is reflected in everything they do: in their costumes, their folklore, their art, even in their homes that are painted using the brightest colours in the spectrum.*

Tea

Given the amount of chai drunk across India today, it is hard to believe that tea (Camellia sinensis) was only introduced to the country from China by the British. Today India is still one of the world's largest tea producers, and the lower slopes of the Western Ghats offer perfect growing conditions. Although the youngest shoots and leaves are used for all varieties, the processing that follows will determine whether they become green tea (light and unfermented), oolong tea (lightly fermented and often scented with flowers, such as jasmine tea), or black tea (strong, fermented). While no tea is harmful, only unfermented green tea, high in powerful anti-oxidants, is actively good for you, with properties said to reduce the likelihood of cancer, cholesterol, cardiovascular disease and strokes, and boost immunity – just for starters.

Some plantations offer tours of the fields and processing plants and even overnight accommodation to visitors. The Indians typically drink their tea strong, very milky and very sweet. At the roadside kiosks, the chai seller will pour the steaming liquid from glass to glass in a high stream to build up a frothy head.

OPPOSITE *You're never far from a cup of chai in the Western Ghats.*

OPPOSITE BELOW *Left to grow freely, tea bushes reach 10 m (32 ft), but to make it easy to pick the new shoots, they are cultivated as flat-topped 1 m (3 ft) tall bushes, planted along the natural contours, leading to this kind of perfectly trimmed landscape.*

RIGHT *Tea pickers wait to have their sacks weighed and checked before they are paid.*

BELOW *Freshly harvested tea leaves must be dried for 24 minutes. This stops the enzyme processes, brings the moisture content down and prevents fermentation.*

LEFT *Tea harvesting is a laborious task that requires some training in order to yield the best results. When plucking the leaves for high quality tea, only the bud and the second and third leaves are plucked. This is called fine plucking. If more leaves are taken with the bud, it produces a lower quality tea. Sometimes mature leaves are discarded, which effectively prunes the bush. This enables nutrients to get into the bush's system and helps with new growth.*

THE NATURAL WORLD

LEFT *A solitary tree is silhouetted against the sky.*

BELOW *Ex-poacher and ace tracker Selvan, who now has a job with the wildlife department, leads a group of tourists into the heart of the Periyar Reserve.*

OVERLEAF *A three-hour ascent from the Yellapatty tea estates takes you to the ridge of the Karankolam Mountains, with the second tallest mountain in the Western Ghats forming a dramatic backdrop.*

Kerala is a naturalist's dream, a state boasting one of the richest varieties of flora and fauna in India. Over 15,000 plant species make up 25 per cent of India's total. Around 100 mammal species include both common and endangered animals, from herds of elephants to the rare Nilgiri langurs, flying lizards and even giant flying squirrels. If you are a dedicated twitcher, you might catch a glimpse of the red-winged cuckoo or the white-bellied tree-pie, but with 550 bird species you are bound to see something new. And to cap it all, 169 reptile species inhabit the wetlands.

Three major national parks and a large number of wildlife and bird sanctuaries cover much of the countryside. The Periyar Wildlife Sanctuary is one of the largest wildlife reserves in India. It was declared a tiger reserve in 1978, and is also known for its herds of wild elephants which you can view from the safety of a boat in the lake. The Eravikulam National Park near Munnar has more than half the world population of the endangered goat species, the Nilgiri tahr. The Silent Valley National Park is thought to be the only surviving bit of evergreen forest in the Sahya Ranges. It's as close to a Garden of Eden as you could hope to get.

Flora

Kerala abounds in 'green magic', with the state's notable biodiversity concentrated in the east. It is estimated that the flora of Kerala comprises around 10,000 species, which include cryophytes, lichens, algae and fungi. Out of the 3,500 species of flowering plants, 900 are highly sought after as medicinal plants.

In Kerala, western allopathic medicine is reserved for emergencies. The Malayali have little faith in modern day medicine, not surprising when there are a wealth of natural remedies to choose from: turmeric and sanjeevini for wounds; natural insulin from the plant Costus igneus for diabetes; the juice from the leaves of Cryptolepis buchanani for healing fractures; the paste made from land daisies for stretch marks – the list is endless. Even the humble coconut has at least ten medicinal uses. Kerala has Ayurvedic remedies for everything from the common cold to cancer. Unfortunately, this has also led to a rapid decline in the population of medicinal plants.

Kerala's mountain slopes also harbour many rare species of orchid, and flowers like the neelakurinji that bloom once in twelve years. Rapid destruction of habitat, due to commercial logging and the growing demands of cultivators, continuously threatens these Xanadus.

ABOVE *These tough, woody, shelf-like bracket fungi grow on the trunks of dead trees in the Western Ghats. Ring growth in the upper surface shows that they can reach ages of 50–70 years.*

LEFT *The neelakurunji (Strobilanthus kunthiana) flowers only once every 12 years, carpeting the hills around the Periyar River. The local Muduvar tribe calculates its age by the flower's blossom. Reportedly, only a tenth of the plants that bloomed in 1982 still remain.*

LEFT *One of nature's cruel ironies, these colourful parasitic plants absorb nutrients from their host plants by means of specialized roots. When their host dies, they move on to another tree.*

BELOW *A lichen is not a single organism, but a partnership between a fungus and an algae. Dry lichen can quickly absorb from 3 to 35 times its weight in water, even absorbing moisture from dew, fog, or from the air itself.*

Insects

Three out of every four living organisms is an insect. This makes them the most numerous, if not the most dominant, group of organisms on earth. Insects also play an important role in the sustenance of the biosphere. Upset their habitat and their population, and it starts a cascade effect. From the conservationist's point of view, the ant is as important as the elephant.

Kerala's forests show a healthy abundance of creepy-crawlies. The Kerala Forest Research Institute has a collection of about 3,000 insect species from different forest habitats, of which only 900 have been authentically identified. It is estimated that when they finally finish cataloguing all that they have found, there will be at least 6,000 insect species in Kerala. So far, however, many species remain unreported or unidentified. In a recent study of the butterflies and moths of Silent Valley, 95 species of butterflies and 318 species of moths were collected. 87 remain unidentified, despite help from London's International Institute of Entomology.

At the more beautiful end of the spectrum, there are at least 330 species of butterfly, of which 37 are endemic to the region, with one of them, the Ghats birdwing (Troides minos) having a wingspan of a staggering 25 cm (10 in). Lepidopterists salivate as they flock to Kerala from across the world.

BELOW LEFT *These dragonflies (Neurothemis tullia) can be commonly seen on the banks of Periyar Lake.*

OPPOSITE *This Crocothemis servilia male is often seen near ponds and streams. They are bright red in colour and the wings are transparent, sometimes with a red patch on the base. Males are more common than females who frequent water bodies only at the time of mating. The nymphs feed primarily on mosquito larvae.*

OPPOSITE BELOW LEFT *Many hundreds of vividly coloured butterflies brighten up the forest floors and fields.*

OPPOSITE BELOW RIGHT *This chocolate pansy butterfly (species Nymphalidae) had been in the wars, surviving an encounter with a predator but damaging its wings.*

Birds

With such a range of habitats to choose from, Kerala is prime bird real estate, with some 500 species on show – it's paradise for bird watchers. Although Kerala's wetlands have shrunk considerably in recent years, they still boast a diverse array of water birds. Kumarakonam Bird Sanctuary hosts ducks, terns, herons and egrets, besides many migratory species that pay a visit every winter. The best time to visit the wetlands is between November and March.

The Western Ghats, which are comparatively protected, harbour many rare species such as the Sri Lanka frogmouth, the oriental bay owl, and large frugivores like the great hornbill and Indian grey hornbill. Other common species include the peafowl, Indian cormorant, jungle and hill myna, oriental darter, black-hooded oriole, greater racket-tailed and black drongoes, bulbul, many species of kingfisher and woodpecker, jungle fowl, Alexandrine parakeet, and assorted ducks and migratory birds.

OPPOSITE ABOVE *Local lizards are not safe with 17 species of owl out hunting across Kerala.*

OPPOSITE BELOW *Unusually, a cormorant's feathers are not waterproof, which helps them to dive fast but means they need to hang their wings out to dry after fishing.*

ABOVE *Native to India, the forest-dwelling peacock is the national bird and considered to be lucky, associated with protection and the goddess Indra.*

RIGHT *A cormorant starts its day with a little wing dance in Periyar.*

Animals

For a relatively small state, Kerala offers an extraordinarily wide range of habitats from evergreen rainforest and highland deciduous forests in the east to the coastal wetlands. Together they provide homes for a hugely rich array of wildlife. Little has survived the intensive development of the plains, but Kerala encompasses 9,400 sq km (3,629 sq miles) of natural forests, which includes the vast highlands of the Nilgiri Biosphere Reserve.

The evergreen rainforests play host to major fauna such as the Asian elephant, Bengal tiger, leopard, Nilgiri tahr, and grizzled giant squirrel. There are thought to be about 40 tigers in Periyar National Park, the best known of the state's reserves. More remote preserves, which include the Silent Valley National Park and the Nilgiri Biosphere Reserve, harbour other endangered species such as the lion-tailed macaque, Indian sloth bear, and gaur. Other common species include water buffalo, porcupine, chital, sambar, langur, flying squirrel, boar, a variety of simians, grey wolf, and the common palm civet. Many reptiles such as the king cobra, viper, monitor lizard, python, turtle, and crocodile are also to be found in Kerala.

OPPOSITE ABOVE *Water buffalo are used for milk, meat and as beasts of burden.*

OPPOSITE BELOW *Most of the world's surviving wild population of Bengal tigers live in India. Periyar is one of a handful of Project Tiger reserves dedicated to their preservation.*

RIGHT *Not a single animal to be seen for five hours, and then a deer ran out of the forest.*

BELOW *The numbers of endangered Nilgiri tahr primitive wild goats are now rising, protected in Eravikulam National Park.*

ELEPHANTS

The Elephant Junction in Thekkady is a paradise for lovers of these wonderful animals, and it is one of the few places where visitors can interact closely with the gentle giants.

The latest star at Elephant Junction is less than 1 m (3 ft) tall, has baby pink toes, and drinks 12 litres (2.6 gallons) of milk a day. Kanan is just nine days old, but has the kind of fan following that any elephant would envy. His caretaker is a patient old *mahout* (handler) who Kanan tries to push over very unsuccessfully at any opportunity that arises. But the baby elephant has already learnt that stomping on peoples' toes is the best way to grab their attention. The old *mahout* wears shoes these days, and a plaster cast on one toe.

LEFT *Elephants understand hundreds of visual and vocal commands. When Laxmi's mahout (handler) asked her to raise her left hind leg, she immediately obliged and was rewarded with a lump of jaggery (raw sugar).*

FAR LEFT AND BELOW *Captured rogue elephants are frequently sent to an elephant training school where they are forced to learn some manners. This tusker used to wreak havoc in villages bordering Tamil Nadu, before he was finally captured. Here he enjoys his bath under the supervision of a trained foster mother and a mahout with a bamboo spear.*

OVERLEAF *The training of a captive elephant generally starts when the elephant reaches four years of age. The working elephant has to spend five years or more in 'elephant school' before it can be assigned to a timber yard. Badly trained elephants have often turned wild and killed their handlers.*

RELIGION

Only around 56 per cent of Keralans are Hindu, and temple culture and architecture here are totally different to those even in neighbouring Tamil Nadu. Non-Hindus are not allowed into the inner sanctum. Even male devotees have to wear the *dhoti* and remove their shirts and vests before entering the temple (probably historically imposed to ensure that weapons could not be carried into the temple). The most famous religious group in the state are the Jews, although after thousands of years, most left for Israel after World War II and only a handful now remain as guardians of their ancient heritage in Kochi.

When the Portuguese set off around the world, Catholic evangelism was nearly as important to them as trade, so they were astonished when they arrived on the Malabar Coast in 1498 to find a long-settled community of Christians. The Apostle Thomas (Doubting Thomas) had got here first, in 52 AD. He established seven churches, in Malankara, Palayur, Paravoor, Kokkamangalam, Niranam, Chayal and Kollam, before being martyred by a fanatic at Little Mount, Mylapore, on 19th December, 72 AD. Today, there are around 9 million Christians in Kerala, with several different churches – Orthodox, Catholic, Protestant and Evangelical – competing for custom. Islam was first introduced to the region peacefully by Arab traders in the late 7th century. Many were encouraged to settle and marry local women by the Zamorin of Calicut, who eventually converted himself. Many of the *dalit* (untouchables) also chose to convert to escape their karma and improve their lot.

So far, all these often fractious religions have manage to survive reasonably happily side by side, although modern pressures such as fundamentalist Islam and pressure against the relative freedom of women in the region threaten centuries of harmony.

LEFT *Spice stalls crowd around the traditional Hindu Suchindram temple, with its sculpted gopuram (tower) telling the great legends.*

ABOVE *Our Lady of Lourdes Metropolitan Cathedral in Trissur Town boasts the tallest church tower in Asia. The church's centenary was celebrated during the visit of Pope John Paul II in 1986.*

RIGHT *Kochi's Paradesi Synagogue dates back to 1568 but was rebuilt in 1662. Elaborate furnishings include gold crowns given as gifts, 10th century copper privileges written in Tamil by Cochin's ruler, old Testament scrolls and Chinese tiles.*

OPPOSITE ABOVE *Christianity's ancient presence in Kerala is visible everywhere. Churches of all shapes and sizes from the simple to the bizarre, such as this tower in Munnar, loom over the landscape.*

OPPOSITE BELOW LEFT *The Santa Cruz Basilica is one of the oldest churches in India, started in 1505 under Francesco de Almeida, the first Portuguese viceroy in India. It was destroyed during the British conquest, rebuilt and consecrated on November 19, 1905. Pope John Paul II raised it to the status of a Basilica in 1984.*

OPPOSITE BELOW RIGHT *The walls and ceiling of the Santa Cruz Basilica are covered with somewhat lurid biblical paintings and painted sculptures of Christ.*

RIGHT *Blessed Kuriakose Elias Chavara was the co-founder and first prior-general of the congregation of the 'Carmelites of Mary Immaculate' and the 'Sisters of the Mother of Carmel'. Many miracles were attributed to him, and by the age of thirty, he was a rising star of Christendom. A keen educationalist, he was also instrumental in setting up the first Catholic printing press, and the first Catholic Sanskrit school. Beatified in 1986 by Pope John Paul II at Kottayam, Kerala, the promise of miracle cures draws hundreds to his shrine.*

ABOVE *Keralan temples are very different architecturally to those elsewhere, with the sanctum set at the centre of a large courtyard surrounded by other low mandapas (halls) with clay-tiled roofs, guarded in turn by high stone walls. Non-Hindus are rarely allowed to visit the sanctum.*

LEFT *Ceremonial lamps in the compound of Calicut Tali Temple are lit at sundown before the prayer rituals begin.*

RIGHT *In a desperate attempt to appease the gods, pilgrims trek great distances with a few basic belongings balanced on their heads in the fond hope that their arduous journey will make their gods a little more generous.*

BELOW RIGHT *This holy man at Ambalapura temple showered blessings on all who crossed his path for a few coins. He also warned the parsimonious about the consequences of bad karma.*

OVERLEAF *In India, every body of water sited close to a place of worship attains sanctity. All sacred pools, according to legend, have their sources in the heavens or the netherworld and have the power to cleanse guilt and cure illness. Invariably, on holy days, when the stars, astrologers and planets are in perfect conjunction, the gods (or demons) decide to risk bathing in the polluted waters.*

PERFORMING ARTS

L ife in Kerala shimmers with music and dance, colour and movement, some of it seemingly as ancient as the land itself and all of it pregnant with meaning. By far the best known of the many dance forms in the state is Kathakali, but others such as Theyyam and Padayani stretch back thousands of years to pre-Hindu Dravidian animist worship. Many other folk dances are still danced in the fields.

Most of the music is bound up with the dance, but while drummers thunder out praise to the gods, the British left their mark with classical European music – Calicut has a flourishing symphony orchestra and choir – and Malayalam movies (a thriving sub-section of Bollywood) have created their own brand of pop.

Kalaripayattu is believed to be one of the oldest forms of martial art, probably dating back to the 5th century AD. It underwent a period of decline after the introduction of firearms, especially after the establishment of British colonial rule in the 19th century, but a resurgence of public interest in Kalaripayattu began in the 1920s in Tellicherry. Mastering the art takes at least ten years and initiation generally starts at the tender age of seven.

Mohiniyattam, Kerala's Indian classical dance tradition danced only by women, developed from devotional dance in the temples, and was designed to symbolize the beauty of cosmic truth to the masses.

OPPOSITE BELOW *The choir of the CSI church enjoys great popularity. Their voices are angelic, the hymns well chosen, and a huge church organ ensures that nobody sleeps through the service.*

ABOVE *A rare tribal form of ritual dance in northern Kerala, Theyyam is linked with ancient Brahmin cults that included worship of the Mother Goddess and nature spirits. A performance, usually held at village shrines, would last for up to 24 hours, with breaks for rituals.*

LEFT *Kalaripayattu draws inspiration from the movements of animals, and its influence can be seen in all the major classical art forms of Kerala, especially in Kathakali.*

Kathakali

The most famous of the classical dance-dramas of Kerala, Kathakali is an all-male production. A Kathakali actor uses immense concentration, skill and physical stamina, gained from training based on Kalaripayattu, the ancient martial art of Kerala, to prepare for his role. The intensive training can last for eight to ten years. Actors do not speak, but dance and mime the *padams* sung by singers. Traditionally there are 101 classical Kathakali stories, based on traditional Indian mythology. Most plays were initially composed to last a whole night. Today, concise versions of the stories (two to four hours, selecting the most popular portions) are increasingly popular.

One of the most interesting aspects is its elaborate make-up code. Mostly the make-up can be classified into five basic sets: *pacha*, *kathi*, *kari*, *thaadi* and *minukku*. The differences between these sets are the predominant colours applied on the face. Green depicts nobility, reds depict evil, women and ascetics have lustrous yellowish faces, while some demons and hunters wear black make-up.

BELOW *Kathakali make-up is made from various mineral pigments. They are ground on a pestle and mixed with coconut oil before being applied to the face. Some characters also have their features enhanced, such as an enlarged nose or an elaborate moustache, or the saucer-like white beard built up from rice paste.*

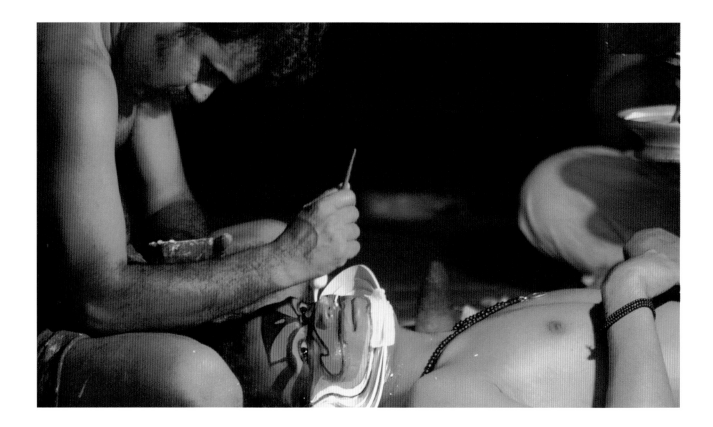

ABOVE LEFT *In Kathakali, the story is enacted by using hand gestures and body movements (mudras) and by facial expressions (rasas). In this scene, an actor mimics a butterfly drinking nectar.*

ABOVE RIGHT *Here Panchali, played by a male actor, searches longingly for her husband Bhima who has gone to collect flowers.*

RIGHT *The curtain falls... and Bhima gets ready to battle tyrants.*

OVERLEAF *Actors play out a scene while a singer narrates a ballad.*

113

FESTIVALS

Snake boats, elephants with umbrellas, cross-dressing dancers and demon kings – when Kerala celebrates, which it does regularly, it does so in fabulously flamboyant style. The biggest festival of the year is Onam, held in August or September in honour of King Mahabali. The legendary demon king was just and good and once a year he returns to check on his people, welcomed with feasts, carpets of flowers, processions and dancing. The festivities leading up to the big day last over a week and include another of the region's great attractions, the *chundanvallam* (snake boat) races in the Backwaters, with the Nehru Trophy in Alleppey (Alappuzha) as the biggest draw. Each boat contains up to 100 oarsmen in banks of two, the rhythm maintained by a chanting cox in the curved prow. Other boat races are held throughout the year.

Even more spectacular than the boats, however, are the various temple festivals of which the Thrissur Pooram in April or May is the most magnificent, with the neighbouring temples at Thiruvambadi and Paramekkavu battling it out as to which can lay on the greatest splendour in its parade of caparisoned elephants, ranks of drummers, torchlight processions and firework displays. Vishu, the Hindu new year (April–May), is celebrated solemnly within the home, although the western new year is celebrated with a huge carnival in Kochi. Deepavali (Diwali, the Festival of Lights) is celebrated with feasting, lights and firecrackers. With nearly half the population either Christian or Muslim, other major religious festivals are also celebrated with gusto – and everyone joins in. It is not uncommon to see plastic Father Christmases on show (celebrated twice for western and orthodox traditions), with banana trees doing duty as Christmas trees and carols accompanied by firecrackers. Easter is treated with great solemnity. Of the Muslim festivals, the most widely celebrated are Bakr Id (the Festival of Sacrifice) and Idul Fitr (the Festival of Sweets) at the end of the month-long Ramadan fast.

FAR LEFT *Since Nehru donated a trophy in 1952, several other Indian premiers have done likewise and the snake boat races are hotly competitive.*

LEFT *During temple festivals, Puli Attam is performed by young men who paint their bodies yellow and black, don fangs, head gear with ears, paws with claws and a tail and mimic the ferocious tiger's movements, spurred on by wildly beating drums.*

117

ABOVE *The spectacular Kudamattam ceremony at the Thrissur Pooram involves an exchange of umbrellas by the competing temples. Both temples enter 15 elephants, with new costumes each year.*

LEFT *Some snake boat crews have more of an eye for the cameras than speed – this looks like something straight out of Sinbad.*

ABOVE *Keralan gods like their music loud, and the Chendamelam drum processions at festivals such as Thrissur Pooram are loud enough to shake the soul.*

RIGHT *An ancient ritual dance from the Travancore region of central Kerala, Padayani celebrates rathi (lust), raktham (blood) and lahari (toxic mood), and is thought to have pre-Hindu roots.*

LEFT *Originating in Portuguese times, Kochi Carnival brings in the western new year with a street parade that includes fancy dress competitions, floats — and, of course, elephants.*

BELOW LEFT *Kochi Carnival attracts all sorts, including the cross-dressing hijras from north India, traditionally hired to dance at birth ceremonies and weddings.*

RIGHT *Elephant processions during temple festivals are a must-see. Caparisoned elephants, led by mounted mahouts with colourful canopies, march down the streets accompanied by an entourage of musicians, pundits and throngs of chanting pilgrims.*

OVERLEAF *During an elephant procession the streets are illuminated with a combination of halogen lamps, firecrackers and flaming torches soaked in oil. It is safer to maintain a distance, as it is not unusual for a nervous elephant to go on the rampage.*

PAGES 124–125 *Fireworks are an essential part of any temple festival — the bigger, brighter and louder the better.*

INDEX

Italicised entries indicate photographs.

PHOTOGRAPHIC CREDITS

The author and L & L Media would like to thank the following for their help: Doug Goodman, info@douggoodmanpr.com; the Indian Tourist Office, www.incredibleindia.org; Taj Hotels, Resorts and Palaces www.tajhotels.com.

The principal photographer is Sunil Vaidyanathan, sunilvaidyanathan@yahoo.com.
Anyone photographing India knows that the history, the beautiful people, the chaos and the gorgeous light make for good shots wherever one points one's lens. Sunil's photos have an extra spark. He has a deep love and concern for his country, the passion to travel extensively and an irreverence that provides an edge. A photographer and writer, Sunil Vaidyanathan published his first book at the age of 21. He has also authored *The Heritage Buildings of Bombay, Temples of South India, Ganesha 'The God of India', Colourful India* and *Pilgrimage Places in India*. Some of these books have been the result of research grants from international funding agencies. He has conducted workshops on photography throughout the country for aspiring photojournalists and is currently working on his sixth photo essay 'River Yatra'.
All the photographs in this book were taken by Sunil Vaidyanathan with the exception of those credited below.

Key to locations: t = top; b = bottom; l = left; r = right; tr = top right; br = bottom right. (No abbreviation is given for pages with a single image, or pages on which all photographs are by the same photographer.)

DG	Doug Goodman	**TWG**	Tony Waltham Geopictures		
ITO	India Tourist Office	**VM**	Vinod T Mathew, vinodtmathew@vividfotos.com,		
MJS	Melissa Shales		http://vividfotos.com		
TH	Taj Hotels, Resorts and Palaces				

Back, left to right,			70	t	TWG	94	b	ITO
1st and 4th picture		ITO	72		TH	95	b	ITO
Inside front flap		ITO	73	t	ITO	110	t	ITO
1		ITO	73	b	TH	111	t	ITO
10		TWG	74	t	ITO	116		VM
14		ITO	75	t, bl	TH	117	b	ITO
24/25	t	ITO	75	br	ITO	118	t	VM
24	b	VM	80	b	ITO	118	b	ITO
25		ITO	81	t	DG	119	t	VM
30/31		TWG	91	bl	ITO	119	b	ITO
38	b	ITO	92	t	ITO	120		VM
43	t	TWG	93	t	MJS	124/125		VM
69	b	DG	94	t	MJS			

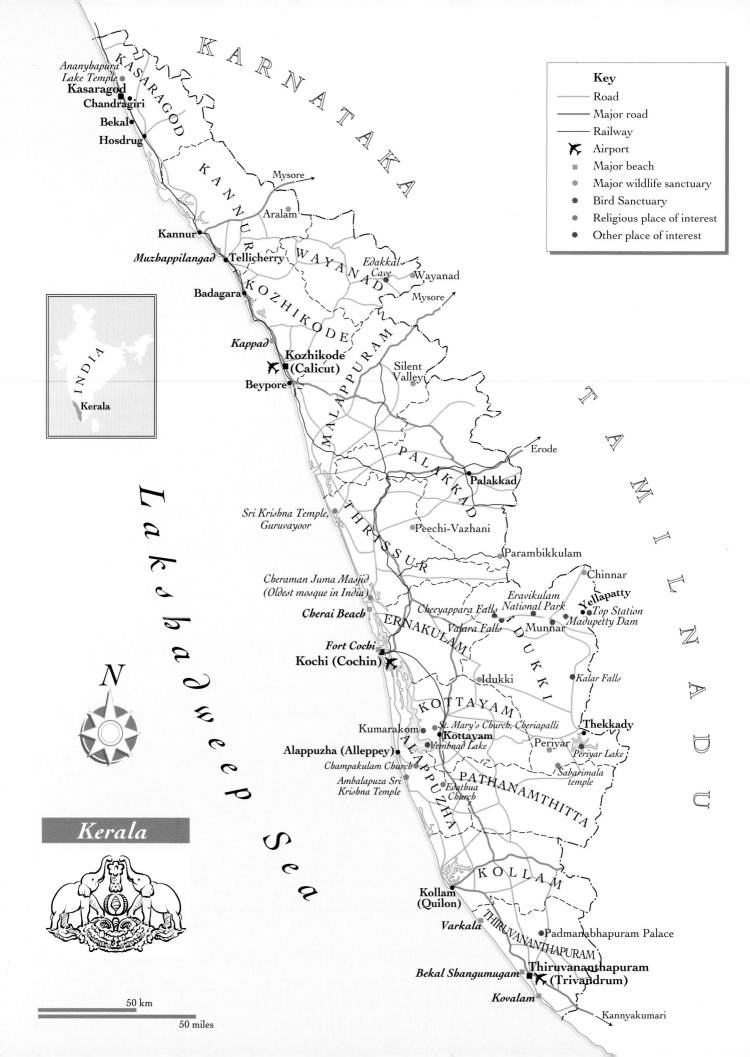